# MACKENZIE'S
# MAGIC  STEAM

Southern Railway's Lord Nelson No. 853 *Sir Richard Grenville*.

# MACKENZIE'S MAGIC STEAM

## As Seen Through A Glass Darkly

## Iain Mackenzie

**Danny Howell Books**
**MCMXC**

*with best wishes*
*Iain Mackenzie*

**Mackenzie's Magic Steam**
**As Seen Through A Glass Darkly**

first published May 1990
by
Danny Howell
57 The Dene, Warminster, Wiltshire, BA12 9ER


Design and Layout Conceived
by
Danny Howell


Typesetting, Photo-screening and Printing
by
Wessex Press Design & Print Limited
Graphic House, 55—57 Woodcock Industrial Estate,
Warminster, Wiltshire, BA12 9DY

Price: £9.99

**ISBN 1 872818 00 5**

# CONTENTS

Acknowledgements . . . . . . . . . . . . . . . . . . . . 6

Introduction . . . . . . . . . . . . . . . . . . . . 7

Population . . . . . . . . . . . . . . . . . . . . 8

4–6–0 . . . . . . . . . . . . . . . . . . . . 9

4–4–0 . . . . . . . . . . . . . . . . . . . . 15

4–4–2 . . . . . . . . . . . . . . . . . . . . 22

2–4–2 . . . . . . . . . . . . . . . . . . . . 27

Singles . . . . . . . . . . . . . . . . . . . . 31

2–4–0 . . . . . . . . . . . . . . . . . . . . 37

0–4–0 . . . . . . . . . . . . . . . . . . . . 41

0–4–2 . . . . . . . . . . . . . . . . . . . . 45

0–4–4 . . . . . . . . . . . . . . . . . . . . 49

0–6–0 . . . . . . . . . . . . . . . . . . . . 51

2–6–0 . . . . . . . . . . . . . . . . . . . . 57

2–6–2 . . . . . . . . . . . . . . . . . . . . 63

2–6–4 . . . . . . . . . . . . . . . . . . . . 67

4–6–4 . . . . . . . . . . . . . . . . . . . . 69

4–6–2 . . . . . . . . . . . . . . . . . . . . 72

0–8–0 . . . . . . . . . . . . . . . . . . . . 77

2–8–0 . . . . . . . . . . . . . . . . . . . . 80

0–10–0 . . . . . . . . . . . . . . . . . . . . 85

0–4–4–0 . . . . . . . . . . . . . . . . . . . . 87

About the author . . . . . . . . . . . . . . . . . . . *Facing page* 88

# ACKNOWLEDGEMENTS

I am grateful for the assistance given to me on London & North Western Railway matters by Mr R. H. Linnell whose knowledge of the subject would make a book in itself.

I have gleaned other information from:—

*Locomotives of The L.N.E.R.* Published by the R.C.T.S.

*The ABC British Railways Locomotives* published by Ian Allan.

*British Steam Locomotives In Colour* by O. S. Nock.

*Locomotives of The L.M.S. Past & Present* by The Locomotive Publishing Company.

*In Search Of Steam 1962–68* by Robert Adley.

I also offer my sincere thanks to Danny Howell for agreeing to publish this book; Wessex Press Design & Print Limited for their help and assistance; Brian Hobson for his photographic work; and Barry Mole for taking the photograph of myself.

*Dedicated to Chris who doesn't remember steam*

# INTRODUCTION

*Magic Lantern: an optical instrument throwing a magnified image of a glass mounted picture on to a white screen in a darkened room*

The *Concise Oxford Dictionary* thus describes this valuable visual aid used by lecturers at the turn of the century. Made of sheet metal, the typical magic lantern measured some 18″ long by 12″ high by 9″ wide; it had a lens and slide carrier at one end and an ornamental chimney on the top. The chimney was vital as it allowed to escape the enormous amount of heat generated by the light source contained within the metal box. Electric light bulbs of the period were incapable of providing sufficient illumination and it was therefore necessary to use an arc lamp to provide the light. This was a pair of carbon rods, which when charged with electricity produced a brilliant white light. Similar lamps were in use in the theatres at that time.

Magic lanterns were large, like the cameras needed to produce the plate glass photographs for use with them. Special plates were employed to provide a positive image suitable for projection, the emulsion side of the plate being sandwiched between a clear sheet of thin glass to protect it from damage, edged with a passe-partout to hold the two sheets together. The completed slide usually measured three and a quarter inches square by one tenth of an inch thick.

This book features 100 photographs of British steam engines taken from magic lantern slides. It is to be regretted that colour photography was not available in those early days. How very much more interesting it would have been to have recorded in pictures the different liveries of the locomotives and rolling stock of the pre-grouping railway companies. The shining brass and copper work together with the intricate lining and lettering cannot be fully appreciated when photographed in black and white. Nevertheless, an idea of the standard of cleanliness maintained by the old railways together with the enormous variety of locomotive and rolling stock designs of those far-off days can be appreciated in these photographic studies on glass.

To the motor car enthusiast there is a vast difference between, say, a Ford Anglia and an Austin Ruby Saloon; a Sunbeam Talbot and a Standard 8. So it is for the railway enthusiast who instantly recognises the difference in outline between a Great Western Railway Castle Class and a Southern Railway King Arthur. Not only are the shapes different but the sounds that they produce when working distinguish one from the other. As with the modern motor car there is very little to identify one make from another, the diesel and electric railway engines have reduced them to a sameness that does little to inspire real interest.

I am fortunate to have had handed down to me a collection of some 400 magic lantern slides recording those halycon days before the arrival of the modern forms of traction. There are but two studies of the first L.M.S. diesel engines and one of an obscure petrol engine shunting locomotive; the remainder are devoted entirely to the steam engine. Depicted are those elderly work horses condemned to the cutter's torch 70 to 80 years ago, down to the many steam giants which shared the same fate in the total destruction of all things steam in the 1960s. Together they provide a valuable insight into the development of the locomotive over the years, to the hundreds of different types that have operated on our railway system, and last but by no means least, supply an aid to the memories of those of us fortunate enough to have worked with these most fascinating of machines – the steam engine, as seen through a glass, darkly.

Iain Mackenzie
May 1990

**Author's note:**

For readers not having a knowledge of certain technical terms used to describe locomotive types, the following explanations may be helpful:

The Whyte system of locomotive classification is the one most generally used in the United Kingdom and specifies the number of carrying and driving wheels. 4–6–2 describes an engine having a bogie (4 wheels) at the leading end, 6 coupled driving wheels, and a pony truck (2 wheels) under the cab. The wheels of the tender are disregarded. A capital letter T following the notation indicates a tank engine, i.e. a locomotive having no separate vehicle carrying coal and water, thus: 4–6–2T.

In addition to this, some wheel arrangement types have also been given names. The following list describes those common to British Railways.

| | |
|---|---|
| 4–4–2 | Atlantic |
| 4–6–2 | Pacific |
| 2–6–0 | Mogul |
| 2–6–2 | Prairie |
| 2–8–2 | Mikado |
| 2–8–0 | Consolidation |
| 4–6–4 | Baltic |
| 0–10–0 | Decapod |

# POPULATION

A census of steam engines taken in March 1955 gives a total of 14,580 locomotives, of which 8,386 were tender engines and 6,194 were tank engines. By far the larger number of units in the fleet of any one wheel arrangement was the ubiquitous 0–6–0 with a total on all regions of 3,178; the London Midland Region alone having 1,460 mostly of ex-Midland Railway origin. The second most numerous type of tender engine was the 4–6–0 which appeared in many shapes and sizes from many builders throughout the British Isles. In 1894 David Jones, of the Highland Railway, introduced the type to Britain with his celebrated Jones' Goods. Very many variants of the type made their appearance over the years until the final designs emerged from Doncaster and Brighton in 1951.

## STEAM LOCOMOTIVES IN SERVICE ON BRITISH RAILWAYS, 26th MARCH 1955

| | | W.R. | L.M.R. | E.R. | S.R. | B.R. | Total |
|---|---|---|---|---|---|---|---|
| Pacific | 4–6–2 | — | 50 | 202 | 140 | 66 | 458 |
| | 4–6–0 | 669 | 1155 | 591 | 165 | 205 | 2785 |
| Baltic | 4–6–4 | — | — | 1 | — | — | 1 |
| Prairie | 2–6–2 | — | — | 186 | — | — | 186 |
| Mogul | 2–6–0 | 217 | 575 | 244 | 174 | 138 | 1348 |
| | 0–6–0 | 124 | 1460 | 1344 | 250 | — | 3178 |
| | 4–4–0 | 23 | 401 | 280 | 150 | — | 854 |
| Atlantic | 4–4–2 | — | — | — | — | — | 5 |
| | 2–4–0 | — | — | 13 | — | — | 13 |
| Consolidation | 2–8–0 | 199 | 674 | 390 | — | 733 | 1986 |
| | 0–8–0 | — | 314 | 135 | — | — | 449 |
| | 2–10–0 | — | — | — | — | 122 | 122 |
| Decapod | 0–10–0 | — | 1 | — | — | — | 1 |

Tender engines, total: 8386

| | | W.R. | L.M.R. | E.R. | S.R. | B.R. | Total |
|---|---|---|---|---|---|---|---|
| Pacific | 4–6–2T | — | — | 97 | 5 | — | 102 |
| | 4–8–0T | — | — | 12 | 4 | — | 16 |
| Consolidation | 2–8–0T | 151 | — | — | — | — | 151 |
| Mikado | 2–8–2T | 54 | — | — | — | — | 54 |
| | 0–8–4T | — | — | 5 | — | — | 5 |
| | 0–8–0T | — | — | 12 | 8 | — | 20 |
| | 0–6–0PT | 1198 | — | — | — | — | 1198 |
| | 0–6–0ST | 15 | 108 | 174 | — | — | 297 |
| | 0–6–0T | 6 | 655 | 543 | 78 | — | 1282 |
| | 0–6–2T | 68 | 18 | 494 | 117 | — | 697 |
| Prairie | 2–6–2T | 394 | 209 | 92 | — | 75 | 770 |
| | 2–6–4T | — | 645 | 100 | 15 | 131 | 891 |
| | 2–4–2T | — | 36 | 52 | — | — | 88 |
| | 2–4–0WT | — | — | — | 3 | — | 3 |
| Atlantic | 4–4–2T | — | 23 | 98 | 3 | — | 124 |
| | 0–4–2T | 95 | — | 4 | — | — | 99 |
| | 0–4–4T | — | 98 | 69 | 207 | — | 374 |
| | 0–4–0T | 15 | 46 | 58 | 14 | — | 133 |
| Beyer-Garrett | 2–6–0+0–6–2 | — | 29 | — | — | — | 29 |
| | 2–8–0+0–8–2 | — | — | 1 | — | — | 1 |

Tank engines, total: 6194

Compiled from *The ABC British Railways Locomotives*, Ian Allan

# 4–6–0

**1.**  J. G. Robinson of the Great Central Railway designed a 4–6–0 in 1903 and an identically outlined 4–4–2 to be used as a comparison between the two types. Class 8C No. 196 was one of the two 4–6–0 engines built by Beyer-Peacock and remained the sole examples of the class, the 4–4–2 being selected for multiplication and these eventually numbered 27 in the Class 8B. The 4–6–0's became L.N.E.R. Class B1 (later B18) and the 4–4–2's Class C4.

**2.**  The mammoth 330 Class of the London & South Western Railway's Dugald Drummond caused quite a stir in railway circles when they appeared in 1905. With their 5' 6" diameter boiler pitched at 9' 0" above rail level they were locomotives of massive proportions. It seems, however, that the design was not particularly successful as the class of five engines spent most of their lives in ''moth balls'' instead of working between Salisbury and Exeter as intended.

**3.** The first Claughton was built by the L.N.W.R. at Crewe in 1913 to the design of C. J. Bowen-Cooke. Originally intended to have large boilers, weight restrictions imposed by the Civil Engineer made the fitting of smaller boilers necessary. These restrictions were relaxed by the L.M.S. Civil Engineer and some of the Claughtons received larger boilers from 1928 onwards. Driving on the leading axle from all four cylinders, they were a remarkable machine when carefully fired and were capable of lifting a 440 ton train up Shap unassisted. No. 1914 *Patriot* was the War Memorial engine to the employees of the L.N.W.R. who died in the Great War 1914–18.

**4.** In 1908 there emerged from the Horwich Works of the Lancashire & Yorkshire Railway a most impressive 4–6–0 designed by George Hughes, they were his Class 8's (also known as Dreadnoughts) but unfortunately their appearance belied their efficiency as they soon acquired the reputation of being "the world's worst". After drastic rebuilding undertaken in 1920 they became considerably improved and took their place alongside the L.N.W.R. Claughtons when that railway merged with the L & Y in 1922. Although the Dreadnoughts were extremely powerful machines they had voracious appetites, consuming 60% more coal per mile than the Castle Class on the Great Western. Pictured above is No. 50455.

**5.** G. J. Churchward's well tried Star Class on the Great Western was used as the basis for an even better locomotive in the shape of the Castles which commenced building at Swindon in 1923. C. B. Collett added larger boiler and cylinders, and an improved cab, to produce a design so successful that Castles were still being built at Swindon 25 years later, albeit with modern embellishments, but the basic principal remained unchanged. No. 4078 *Pembroke Castle* is seen here with original large chimney and 3,500 gallon tender.

**6.** An acute shortage of express locomotives on the L.M.S. in the late 1920's caused them to cast envious eyes towards the enormously successful Great Western Castles, so much so that they approached Swindon with a view to purchasing some of their 4–6–0's. When these overtures were refused the L.M.S. turned to the Southern Railway whose new Lord Nelson Class were then the most powerful 4–6–0's in the country. No. 862 *Lord Collingwood* was one of the class of 16, the drawings of which were loaned to the L.M.S. drawing office.

**7.** The use of the Southern Railway's Lord Nelson drawings combined with the expertise of the North British Locomotive Co., enabled Sir Henry Fowler's design team at Derby to produce a much needed express passenger 4–6–0 for the L.M.S. The first 25 of these new engines were given regimental names hence the class becoming known as the Royal Scots. The remaining members of the series were provided with names associated with early historical locomotives but these were later renamed to bring them into a uniform naming policy. No. 6137 *Vesta* later became *The Prince of Wales Volunteers (South Lancashire)*. The Scots were an immediate success and coped admirably with the heavy passenger trains plying between Euston and the North.

**8.** The light track foundations and underline bridges on the Great Eastern Railway presented problems for the locomotive engineer until the end of steam in the 1960's. At the turn of the century trains were becoming consistently heavier but there were strict limitations on the size of the engines that could be provided to haul them. S. D. Holden built his 1500 Class light enough but with sufficient power to cope with the weight of the trains. They first appeared in 1911 and proved to be strong, capable machines. Pictured is the No. 8558 built by Beardmore & Co., in 1921. They were later classified B12 by the L.N.E.R. and many were rebuilt and modernised.

**9.** In 1927, Nigel Gresley, of the L.N.E.R., still hampered by the weight restrictions of the Great Eastern, produced specifications for a modern locomotive which was built by the North British Locomotive Co., in the shape of the B17 Sandringham Class. These engines were named after country estates in territory served by the L.N.E.R. and the first batch ran coupled to the short G.E. type tender. Later versions of the B17's ran coupled to the standard L.N.E. style tender and were named after football teams, hence their being dubbed "Footballers". No. 61636 *Harlaxton Manor* with its G.E. tender is illustrated.

**10.** In 1927, still battling for the biggest and best, C. B. Collett managed to win the title for Swindon which was to remain unbroken for a British 4–6–0 locomotive when No. 6000 *King George V* emerged from the Great Western Works. Compared with the G.E.R's B12's 108 tons 16 cwt engine and tender, the G.W.R. Kings weighed in at 135 tons 14 cwt. It was because of this extreme weight that the Kings were restricted to run over the principal routes from Paddington only. No. 6000 was shipped to the United States after a brief running in period where it ran in the Centenary Celebrations of the Baltimore & Ohio Railroad. It is illustrated fitted with the Westinghouse brake pump for use in the U.S.A., where it also featured a bell to commemorate the event. *King George V* has been preserved by Bulmer's of Hereford and operates occasional steam specials on British Rail metals.

# 4–4–0

Although in the years of the Big Four (1923–1948) the 4–6–0 was a common sight on most passenger trains, the situation was entirely different at the turn of the century when Britain was covered by a mass of small railway companies, not many of which possessed anything as large as a 4–6–0. The wheel arrangement favoured by the railways in those days was the 4–4–0. In 1923 on the L.N.E.R. alone the total number of 4–4–0's in capital stock was 920 engines. By 1955 numbers had dwindled to a mere 256.

**11.** In 1895 J. F. McIntosh was appointed Locomotive Engineer to the Caledonian Railway at St Rollox Works in Glasgow. He became well known for his 4–4–0 Dunalastair Classes there being initially three series all having 6' 6" driving wheels, the 15 engines in each series being improvements upon those in the previous builds which took place between 1896 and 1899. The fourth and final Dunalastairs appeared in 1904 and were provided with larger boilers. The Dunalastair IV's were still running on the Scottish Region in 1955. Dunalastair was the name of the Caledonian Railway Chairman's country seat.

**12.** For the opening of the Great Central Railway's London Extension in 1899 a series of 33 4–4–0's were constructed by Gorton Works and Beyer-Peacock to the design of Harry Pollitt. Given the classification 11A by the G.C.R. they later became D6's when taken into L.N.E.R. stock in 1923. The first passenger train to depart from the newly opened Marylebone Station on March 9th 1899 was hauled by one of these 4–4–0's. In 1902 the 11A's were displaced from main line duties and were re-employed on secondary services in the Chester/Liverpool areas where they continued to do excellent work. No. 870 was withdrawn by the L.N.E.R. in 1931.

**13.** North Eastern Railway Class R (L.N.E.R. Class D20) designed by Wilson Worsdell and built at Gateshead in 1900. They were an extremely reliable machine and when first introduced worked the principal expresses between Newcastle and Edinburgh, Newcastle and Leeds.

**14.** Named locomotives were something of a rarity on some pre-grouping railways. No. 1757 *Beatrice,* a Johnson 4–4–0 built in the late 1890's for the Midland Railway was one such.

**15.** The chairman of the Great Eastern Railway was honoured when No.1900 emerged from Stratford Works named *Claud Hamilton*. This was in the year 1900 and it was the first "big" engine to take to the metals on the East Anglian routes from Liverpool Street. They were an extremely efficient locomotive and the original design by James Holden was later improved. No. 62539 above was one of the last of the class (which originally totalled 120) was scrapped in 1960.

**16.** The first examples of H. A. Ivatt's D2 class for the Great Northern Railway were constructed at Doncaster in 1898. In spite of their slender appearance they were capable of hauling some of the heavy trains from King's Cross at remarkable speeds. In later years they were relegated to secondary services in the East Midlands. No. 62172 was the last survivor of the class which originally totalled 70. Scrapping took place in June 1951.

**17.** A familiar sight for commuters at the turn of the century were the Adams' 4–4–0 tank engines which he designed for the North London Railway. First introduced in 1868 they lasted well into the 1920s, working trains from Broad Street into the suburbs of North London.

**18.** On the London Underground, at the same time, the Beyer-Peacock locomotives were working on the Metropolitan and District lines. They could be seen from 1871 until September 1905 when lines they worked were electrified.

**19.** During the years 1873 to 1897 Crewe Works produced more than two dozen different designs from the drawing office of F. W. Webb. The 24th type to appear, in 1897, were the Jubilees named in honour of the Golden Jubilee of Queen Victoria. They were four cylinder compounds, and No. 1922 *Intrepid* was built in 1900. In 1916 it was rebuilt as a two cylinder simple and became a Renown class engine, finally being scrapped in 1927.

**20.** No. 3268 *Chough* was one of William Dean's famous outside framed Duke class built at Swindon in 1896. Originally intended for hauling the G.W.R.'s express trains on the hilly routes beyond Newton Abbot, they continued to be used as assisting power on those routes well into the present century. The Duke of Cornwall class were all given suitable names associated with their West Country location. Chough being a species of crow whose habitat is either mountainous regions or rocky sea coasts.

**21.** In 1902 William Dean was succeeded by George Jackson Churchward at Swindon. Churchward immediately set about the task of standardising locomotive design. 4–6–0s would be used on main line passenger duties and 4–4–0s would be required on routes where the larger engines were prohibited. No. 3814 *County of Chester* was one of the class of 4–4–0's named after counties having connections with the Great Western.

# 4–4–2

4–4–2's were always known as Atlantics and of the 295 tender engines of this type running in Britain, 241 were in use on the L.N.E.R.

**22.** In December 1898 there emerged from the Great Northern Railway's works at Doncaster H. A. Ivatt's Atlantic No. 990, the first 4–4–2 to run in this country. At that period the Gold Rush in the Yukon was creating a great deal of interest and the new locomotives were known throughout their lives as Klondykes. No. 990 was the sole member of the class to receive an official name – *Henry Oakley*. This was a tribute to the former general-manager who had retired in 1896. The Klondykes took over the running of the main line expresses until they were gradually superseded by the larger Atlantics at about the time of the Great War. *Henry Oakley* has been preserved as part of the National Collection.

**23.** In February 1899 the Lancashire & Yorkshire Railway produced their Atlantic, beaten to a "first" by a mere three months by the G.N.R. Aspinall's 1400 Class were very impressive machines and were known as Highfliers in view of their very highly pitched boilers, large 7' 3" wheels and a propensity for very fast running. They lasted until 1933 on the L.M.S.

**24.** The sharply curving routes of the North British Railway radiating from Edinburgh presented serious problems for the locomotive engineer. Engines having long wheel bases could not be satisfactorily employed, therefore the power house had to be packed into a small machine. W. P. Reid's Atlantics were the perfect solution to these difficulties because they were capable of running the heaviest trains on the tightest of schedules with remarkable efficiency. They were given names befitting their locality on the scottish Borders. No. 878 *Hazeldean* became Class C11 on the L.N.E.R. It was built in 1906 and scrapped at the end of 1936.

**25.** Compounding was the "in thing" at the end of the 19th century. Most locomotive engineers tried their hand at it with varying degrees of success. It involved using high and low pressure cylinders on a locomotive whereby the steam could be made to work twice before being exhausted to the atmosphere. G. J. Churchward of the Great Western Railway was greatly impressed by the compounds working on the Northern Railway of France, so much so that he persuaded his directors to purchase a de Glehn compound in 1903 and a further two in 1905. No. 104 was one of the latter. Their use provided valuable data upon which Swindon based its future designs albeit on the simple expansion system.

**26.** London Brighton & South Coast Railway's No. 90 was one of the I3 (pronounced "eye" three) express tank engines designed by Earle Marsh in 1908 for the fast passenger traffic plying between London and Brighton. They were ideal for this purpose, the turn round at each end of the line was simplified as they could run equally well either boiler or bunker first.

**27.** From 1906 to 1909 the L.N.W.R. built a class of 40 Atlantic tank engines designed by George Whale. No. 3044 was built at Crewe during this period.

# 2–4–2

**28.** The 2–4–2 wheel arrangement was devoted almost entirely to tank locomotives. L.N.W.R. No. 768 was built in 1897 and was one of Webb's 4' 6" tanks.

**29.** Great Central Railway's No. 776, Class 9G, which became Class F2 on the L.N.E.R. was one of ten of that type built by Beyer-Peacock & Co., and designed by Pollitt. No. 776 was the first in March 1898 and later became No. 67104 on British Railways. It was scrapped in 1949.

**30.** 20 Class G69s were built at Stratford for the Great Eastern Railway in 1910/11 where S. D. Holden was C.M.E. No. 67 became 7067 on the L.N.E.R. and was classified F6. They could be found on the East Anglian branch lines until dieselisation made them redundant from 1955 onwards.

**31.** The Lancashire & Yorkshire Railway ran a fleet of no less than 330 2–4–2Ts, one of which is No. 227.

**32.** Starting life as a 2–4–0T, on the Metropolitan lines in London, Great Western No. 3593 was converted to a 2–4–2T in 1905.

**33.** Though not strictly speaking a 2–4–2, the eight wheeled 2–2–2–2's of the London & North Western Railway can be included here. F. W. Webb's Greater Britain Class 3 cylinder compounds with divided drive, the inside low pressure cylinder drove onto the second axle and the high pressure cylinder onto the third. To complicate matters still further, the driving wheels were not coupled. No. 526 *Scottish Chief* was built at Crewe in May 1894 and scrapped in 1906 when its name was transferred to a new 4–6–0 Experiment Class.

# Singles

Locomotives with but one driving axle were, perhaps, the most graceful machines ever to run on British railways. With the absence of outside valve gear their huge wheels appeared to glide along quite effortlessly.

**34.** Although the Caledonian Railway had a class of 2–2–2s, they had only one 4–2–2 — Dugal Drummond's famous No. 123 which has fortunately been preserved. This engine took part in the Race To The North in 1888 when the Caledonian paired with the L.N.W.R. for the West Coast Route.

**35.**   No. 667 *Marmion* and 806 *Waverley* were the engines which worked the L.N.W.R.'s portion of the run on alternate days. They were originally designed by John Ramsbottom and were earlier known as Problem Class locomotives. This became changed to Lady Of The Lake after about 1862.Lady Of The Lake Class No. 802 *Red Gauntlett* shows its 7′ 7½″ driving wheels.

**36.**   The challengers on the East Coast route in the Race To The North were the Great Northern, the North Eastern, and the North British Railway companies. The Great Northern ran one of their singles, No. 668, which was perhaps, the most famous of them all. Patrick Stirling provided them with a grace of outline to match their 8′ diameter driving wheels. No. 1 is preserved in the National Collection.

**37.** H. Pollitt produced a design for a 7′ 9″ 4–2–2 for the Great Central Railway, six were built at Gorton in 1900, and No. 969 appeared in August of that year. They all worked initially from Neasden to Leicester on the G.C.'s London Extension. They were later transferred to the Cheshire lines. Classified X4 by the L.N.E.R., they had all been withdrawn by August 1927.

**38.** In 1887 S. W. Johnson turned his attention away from four and six coupled engines, and produced the graceful 4–2–2 for the Midland Railway. They had a tendency to slip imperceptibly and earned themselves the name "Spinners". They were extremely fast and economical machines. Speeds of 90 mph were quite within their capabilities.

**39.** Great Western Railway 2–2–2 *North Star* was a broad gauge (7′ 0½″) locomotive. The original was scrapped in 1906 but a replica was produced for the Railway Centenary celebrations in 1925. It is seen here on its elevated perch in "A" Shop at Swindon Works.

# 2–4–0

**40.** The Midland Railway built a succession of 2–4–0 locomotives, the first of which were the 156 Class appearing in 1866 to the design of Matthew Kirtley. Over the years these engines were rebuilt and modernised as conditions dictated which said much for the outstanding quality of the original design. No. 158 was the third member of the series and was transferred to the duplicate list as No. 158A. It became No. 2 on the Midland Railway in 1907 and 20002 on the L.M.S.R. in 1923. It finally retired from service in 1948 and was restored to its original livery as No. 158A, in which form it can be seen today.

**41.** No. 2003 *Electro* was one of 155 Precedent Class locomotives built at Crewe for the London & North Western Railway from 1874 onwards, the last one appearing in 1901. Francis Webb used for the first time short steam passages in their design making them extremely powerful machines capable of high speeds. One of the class, No. 790 *Hardwicke*, has been preserved and is part of the National Collection.

**42.** No. 167 of Class 12A on the Manchester, Sheffield & Lincolnshire Railway was one of the final batch of 2–4–0s built to Charles Sacre's design in 1885. There were originally 28 locomotives in the class and they worked the fast Manchester to Liverpool expresses of the Cheshire Lines Committee.

**43.** Great Eastern Railway Class T26 later became Class E4 on the L.N.E.R. No. 7435 was originally numbered 435 when it emerged from the Stratford Works in April 1891. The design was by Holden and they were intended for mixed traffic duties in East Anglia. Construction continued in batches until 1902 when the class totalled 100 engines. No. 7435 was scrapped in 1928. Several E4's were handed over to British Railways in 1948; one of these, No. 490, was restored to the Great Eastern Railway blue livery and preserved as part of the National Collection.

**44.** Although not strictly 2–4–0s, F. W. Webb's Experiment Class built 1882–1884 had a leading ponie truck and two uncoupled driving axles making them 2–2–2–0s. They were compound locomotives and the type was further developed through the Dreadnoughts of 1884 to the final class of the type, the Teutonics, built in 1889. The Experiments and the Dreadnoughts were not entirely successful designs. The Teutonics proved to be better machines when Webb included an improved valve gear in their design. In view of their uncoupled driving wheels all three classes proved to be difficult engines to start from rest.

# 0–4–0

**45.** The diminutive Y8 class of the L.N.E.R. began life on the North Eastern Railway in 1890. Designed by T. W. Worsdell, they measured 17' 10½" over buffers, and weighed 15½ tons complete with coal and water. No. 8091 was employed in its early years as one of five of the class shunting in Hull Docks. It was used during its final years as shed shunter at York where it could be seen pushing and pulling engines of 140 tons around the shed yard.

**46.** The Great Eastern Railway acquired a Motor Rail & Tram Co., petrol engined shunting locomotive in 1919 for operating in Lowestoft Docks. It was transferred to Brentford by the L.N.E.R. in 1925 when it was classified Y11 and numbered 8430. It was used to replace horses which were employed in shunting wagons. It too went to the knackers yard in 1956.

**47.** In 1891 The Lancashire & Yorkshire Railway, built a series of 0–4–0 saddle tanks known affectionately as Pugs. They weighed 21 tons five cwt.

**48.** The pugs' counterparts on the Midland Railway were the Deeley 0–4–0 tanks of 1907. 41532 carried its British Railways' number when it was shedded at Burton on Trent.

# 0–4–2

**49.** William Stroudley designed the D1 class tank engines for general local working on London suburban and country branches. They were built at Brighton between 1873 and 1887, the class totalled 125 when completed. No. 34 *Balham* appeared in 1876 and was withdrawn in 1926.

**50.** The London Brighton & South Coast Railway built a number of 0–4–2 classes for express train working. They were very handsome machines with the clean outline of the Stroudley tradition. Their driving wheels were 6' 6" in diameter and the trailing wheels measured 4' 6" in diameter. No. 180 *Arundel* was one of Class B1 and was built in 1890 although the first engine of the class was put into service in 1883. The most famous of the type, No. 214 *Gladstone*, has been preserved and is a part of the National Collection.

**51.** Whilst the L.B.S.C.R. had several different classes of 0–4–2 tender engines, the L.S.W.R. had but one class of that type. They were the Adams' Jubilee class built in the years 1887 and 1895. They worked the fast mixed traffic trains of the South Western. Three of the original class of 90 engines survived until 1948.

**52.** An L.N.W.R. 0–4–2 pannier tank engine which survived into British Railways days was No. 47862. It was originally built at Crewe in 1896 when F. W. Webb was locomotive engineer.

**53.** For light branch work, particularly for "push-pull" activity, the Great Western 1400 class was designed by Charles Collett in 1932. There were 75 engines of the 1400 class which were "push-pull" fitted and 20 engines of the 5800 class which were non-auto engines.

# 0–4–4

**54.** The M7 tank engines were excellent engines and examples of the class lasted for 60 years. Dugald Drummond designed them for the L.S.W.R. and they first appeared in 1897. They ran originally on surburban passenger trains and on country branches. They continued in use on empty coaching stock duties at Waterloo up until the end of steam working.

**55.** Class H No. 31320 was one of Wainwright's 0–4–4 tanks fitted for push-pull working on the South Eastern Railway and was introduced in 1904. One of the class is preserved on the Bluebell Railway.

# 0–6–0

Pehaps the most numerous of all wheel arrangements, the 0–6–0 was used mainly for freight and shunting locomotives, although many could be employed on passenger trains as and when required.

**56.** Over a period of 19 years, commencing in 1873, Crewe Works manufactured a series of 0–6–0s known throughout their lives as the 17″ coal engines. They had 17″ diameter cylinders and 500 were built without change in the design until 1892. In 1880 F. W. Webb produced another 0–6–0 design, this time with 18″ diameter cylinders. These became known as "Cauliflowers" and had the distinctive curved footplate over the driving wheel pins.

**57.** A very large proportion of the goods carried by the Midland Railway was coal from the Nottinghamshire/Derbyshire collieries. To perform these duties a large number of 0–6–0s were constructed at Derby. Most of these were taken into L.M.S. stock in 1923 and many remained to become British Railways property in 1948. No. 58165 was introduced in 1917.

**58.** 175 engines of Great Central Class 9J were built between 1901 and 1910 to the design of J. G. Robinson. They became Class J11 on the L.N.E.R. and were employed on various duties from the lowly pick-up freight to the occasional glory of an express passenger train. They were universally popular among their crews who nick-named them 'Pom-poms' from the sharp, staccato bark of their exhausts. It is to be regretted that none of them survived the cutter's torch, the entire class having succumbed by 1962. No. 64430 is illustrated with its British Railways number.

**59.** The Great Northern Railway Works at Doncaster constructed many 0–6–0s for goods and coal traffic. They were designed by H. A. Ivatt and when taken into L.N.E.R. stock became classes J1 to J6. No. 65481 was one of Class J5 built in 1910 and was scrapped by British Railways in 1953. Most of their lives were spent working in the Nottinghamshire and Derbyshire areas.

**60.** A series of six coupled locomotives built at Brighton for the L.B. & S.C.R. from 1893 onwards were to the design of R. J. Billington and classified C2. They were later modified by D. E. Marsh to give improved performance and were classified C2X. These conversions commenced in 1908 and progressed until 1940.

**61.**   One of the most notable 0–6–0 designs of the late 19th century were the handsome Dean Goods. These engines could be found in service throughout the Great Western Railway and many examples could also be found on other companies' lines when they were on loan from Swindon. During the wars the Railway Operating Division of the Royal Engineers transhipped a large number of these useful machines to be employed in the theatres of war and many never returned to their home ground.

**62.**   The Great Western built an enormous number of 0–6–0PT (pannier tanks) for various shunting and light branch train traffic over their entire network. They numbered in excess of 1300 in 1952 and many variations on the original theme existed at that date. No. 8726 of the 57XX class was designed by C. B. Collett and was introduced at Swindon in 1929.

**63.** The last design of 0–6–0 to appear on British railways was to the design of O. V. Bulleid for the Southern Railway during the Second World War. In order to save extensive use of vital materials at that critical period they were built without the usual embellishments to be found in traditional designs. They were totally unique in their appearance, having no running plate, an unusual shaped boiler, and Bulleid's box-pok wheels. They also carried the new style numbering system which employed a letter to signify the wheel arrangement followed by the actual engine number. No. 33007 appeared as C7 when first built in 1944, "C" representing the six coupled driving wheels. Known to Railwaymen as 'Charlies' they were extremely efficient machines and capable of fast running.

# 2–6–0

This type originated in the United States in the 1840s. 2–6–0s became generally known as moguls, and were built for slow goods work but by the end of the century had ben superseded by much larger machines.

**64.** The L.B.S.C.R. constructed their Class K 2–6–0s between 1913 and 1920. They were built to the design of L. B. Billington and proved to be highly satisfactory engines for hauling the heavy freight trains of the 1914–18 War. Billington prepared drawings for a 2–6–2 freight engine as a development of his Class K but the scheme was not to materialise and a final batch of seven 2–6–0s emerged from Brighton in 1920/21. No. 347 was the first of this final batch.

**65.** Mr H. N. Gresley designed a series of 2–6–0s for the Great Northern Railway, commencing in 1912. The original design was improved from 1914 and further engines were built at Doncaster up until 1921 when the class totalled 67 units. When travelling at speed riding on the footplate could be extremely "lively" and this led to the K2s being given the nickname "Ragtimers". They were used over much of the L.N.E.R. system and the engines allocated to Scotland were named after various highland lochs. No. 61763 was one of the series built in 1918 and spent the last months of its life as a stationary boiler providing steam at a shed in Nottingham before going for scrap in 1961.

**66.** In 1920 H. N. Gresley went on to design a mogul with a 6' 0" diameter boiler and although primarily intended for use on fast freights they were often pressed into service on express passenger trains. Their syncopated beat led them to be nicknamed ''Jazzers'' among enginemen. The K3's totalled 183 when building ceased in 1937, and although prone to rough riding when in a run down condition, they were well liked by their crews. No. 153 was built at Darlington in 1925, was renumbered 1845 by the L.N.E.R. in 1946 and to 61845 by B.R. in 1948. It was scrapped in 1962.

**67.** The Crabs, as the Horwich 2–6–0s came to be called, were designed by George Hughes when he was Chief Mechanical Engineer between 1923 and 1925 but were not introduced until 1926. Their large cylinders made it necessary to raise the footplate at the forward end of the engine which had some bearing on its unusual nickname. They were extremely versatile locomotives and could cope equally well with 75 mph passenger trains or with the long slog of freight trains. No. 42925 was one of the class which totalled 245 engines.

**68.** No. 42969 was one of the 2–6–0s built at Crewe. The prototype which appeared in 1933 was Mr W. A. Stanier's first design for the L.M.S.R. after his appointment as Chief Mechanical Engineer in 1932. Stanier's earlier training at Swindon was apparent in the many G.W.R. features which appeared in his 2–6–0's. They were known variously as Lobsters or Camels.

**69.** The last two designs for the L.M.S.R. before it became part of British Railways were both 2–6–0s and they were both designed by Mr H. G. Ivatt. The smaller locomotive of the two appeared in 1946 and was intended to replace many of the ageing small locomotives on branch lines. Pictured above is No. 46436.

**70.** The other, larger moguls made their debut in 1947 and were to form the basis for the British Railways standard 2–6–0 design to emerge in 1953. Their ungainly appearance earned them the sobriquet Flying Pigs. No. 43044 was one of the class of 162 engines built for mixed traffic duties.

**71.** In 1917 R. E. L. Maunsell designed a general purpose 2–6–0 for the South Eastern & Chatham Railway. The Ashford built prototypes proving to be so successful that the government of the day decreed that a further series of 50 be constructed in kit form by Woolwich Arsenal to alleviate unemployment. This was in 1920/22. Some of these were purchased by the Southern Railway in 1924 and they became known as 'Woolworths' throughout their existance — for Woolwich read Woolworth! They were reliable machines, well liked by their crews and the operating authorities. The last of the N Class as they were officially classified, surviving well into 1966, the end of steam sealing their fate not obsolescence.

# 2–6–2

The 2–6–2 wheel arrangement — generally referred to as "Prairie" — was used mostly on tank locomotives although the L.N.E.R. had a large fleet of tender engines of the type.

**72.** The 1' 11½" gauge Vale of Rheidol Railway, which winds its way up the mountainside between Aberystwyth and Devils Bridge, has almost continuous gradients of 1 in 50 for its entire route. The three 2–6–2T engines which work the line were introduced in 1923 and were designed and built at Swindon. They are numbered 7, 8 and 9, and given suitable Welsh names: *Owain Glyndwr, Llywelyn* and *Prince of Wales*. They were the only narrow gauge engines and the last remaining steam engines to be operated by British Rail, the line having recently been purchased by a private company.

**73.** No. 40178 was one of a class of 139 engines introduced in 1935 by the L.M.S. to the design of W. A. Stanier and was one of his less successful locomotives. They were a taper boiler development of an earlier 2–6–2T with parallel boiler designed by Fowler, of which it was said "Could not raise enough steam to keep the tea urn going in a busy restaurant."

**74. & 75.** In 1955 the Western Region had 391 2–6–2Ts of Great Western origin working on main lines and branches throughout the system. For light branch work the 56½ ton 4400 Class were introduced in 1904, their 4' 1½" driving wheels making them quite distinctive from their larger brethren, the 6100 Class with 5' 8" wheels. Churchward introduced the type in 1904 and from this basic design all the other classes were developed. Wheel sizes changed, boiler pressures increased and detail alterations were made, but the original distinctive Swindon outline remained.

**76.** ''The engine that won the War'' is a phrase that has been used to describe Sir Nigel Gresley's 2–6–2 tender engine, classified V2 by the L.N.E.R.. The prototype engine was named *Green Arrow,* linking the class to the express Green Arrow freight traffic which ran from Kings Cross each evening. They were a scaled down version of the A3 Pacifics and were capable of standing in on express passenger duties on the main lines of the L.N.E.R. They had 6′ 2″ driving wheels and weighed 145 tons in working order. No. 4771 was introduced in 1936 and the class eventually totalled 184. 4771 has been preserved, having run as 60800 on British Railways.

**77.** The final engines of this type to be built in this country were the 84000 Class designed at Derby and introduced in 1953. They were part of the British Railways Standard fleet of locomotives.

# 2–6–4

This wheel arrangement was devoted entirely to tank engines, the type appearing on three of the four post grouping companies — the Great Western being the exception.

**78.** The L.M.S. had a total of 645 2–6–4 tank engines built between 1927 and 1945. The Derby derived Fowler version had Midland origins with parallel boilers, the type was improved in 1933 by W. A. Stanier with the introduction of a taper boilered version. They were employed over the entire L.M.S. system and in later years could be found working semi-fast trains on the other regions of British Railways. No. 42339 above was one of the Fowler engines.

# 4–6–4

The 4–6–4 was a comparatively rare wheel arrangement and only one engine of this type survived to become British Railways property in 1948.

**79.** William Whitelegg designed a massive 4–6–4T engine for the London Tilbury & Southend Railway which was taken over by the Midland in 1912. No. 2102 is illustrated double-heading with a Midland 2–4–0 No. 130.

**80.** The London, Brighton & South Coast Railway built seven 4–6–4Ts to the design of L. B. Billinton for their express passenger train services to the South Coast. With the electrification of the Brighton lines these massive machines were rendered redundant and the Southern Railway rebuilt them as 4–6–0 tender engines. No. 327 *Charles C. Macrae* was built in 1914, was converted in 1935 to form part of the N15X Class, and was renamed *Trevethick*.

**81.** The only 4–6–4 tender engine to run in Britain was built at Darlington for the L.N.E.R. in 1929. Numbered 10000 it was constructed under great secrecy and thus became known as "the Hush Hush". It was equipped with a high pressure marine style boiler operating at 450 lb/sq in, feeding four cylinders for compound working. In this form it ran as an experimental locomotive until rebuilt as an orthodox three cylinder simple in 1937. Taking the form of the more usual wedge fronted streamlining similar to the A4s, it ran without names although proposals were made to call it *Pegasus* soon after it was rebuilt. It was scrapped in 1959.

# 4–6–2

**82.** The first British Pacific type — the name usually applied to engines of the 4–6–2 wheel arangement — was built by the Great Western Railway in 1908 but it remained a solitary machine and was later rebuilt as a 4–6–0. It befell to Mr H. N. Gresley to design a Pacific that proved to be the forerunner of all express engines to run over East Coast routes from 1922 until the demise of steam in 1968. The prototype emerged from Doncaster in 1922, was numbered 1471 and was named *Great Northern*. Classified A1 by the L.N.E.R., members of the class were built and named mostly after famous racehorses. With development and improvements, they were eventually classified A3. *Flying Scotsman* is perhaps the most famous of all engines and is the only surviving member of a class which totalled 78 by the time building ceased in 1935. No. 60062 *Minoru* was built as an A1 in 1925, rebuilt to become A3 in 1944, and withdrawn in 1963. The racehorse *Minoru* after which the engine was named, was the winner of the Derby in 1909.

**83.** 46257 *City of Salford* was the last Pacific to be built at Crewe to an L.M.S. design (it was in fact built in 1948 and was thus a British Railways engine). The first of the class was introduced in 1933 and was to the design of W. A. Stanier. They were responsible for handling the heavy West Coast main line expresses from Euston which they did with the greatest of ease. *City of Salford* had the benefit of modern refinements which the early Duchesses lacked and was thus the ultimate in steam engine design.

**84.** 6227 *Duchess of Devonshire* shows the streamlined version of the Duchess Pacifics which made their appearance when streamlining was in vogue in 1937. The outer casing was later removed to reduce weight and render ease of maintenance. The prototype engine No. 6220 *Coronation* attained a speed of 114 mph on the trial run of the Coronation Scot on 29th June 1937. The first batch of Duchess streamliners were painted in a striking shade of Cambridge blue with horizontal silver stripes. In 1939, later additions to the class were bedecked in crimson lake with gold horizontal stripes.

**85.** The streamlining era produced the record-breaking 4468 *Mallard* built at Doncaster in March 1938. It was followed, two months later, by another A4 No. 4500 named *Garganey,* renamed *Sir Ronald Matthews* in 1939 as a tribute to the Chairman of the L.N.E.R. Board of Directors. It was renumbered 1 in 1946 and 60001 in 1948. The A4s were subjected to a number of colour changes. The first four were painted silver and grey when first built, followed by a period when apple-green was tried as a livery, but the ultimate colour adopted for them was garter blue with deep red wheels.

**86.** When Mr O. V. Bulleid took charge of design on the Southern Railway in 1937, he revolutionised the entire concept of locomotive engineering. At one stroke he produced a steam engine with a great number of totally new ideas. The Merchant Navy Class Pacific appeared in 1941 and its outline alone was a departure from accepted practice; the wheels lacked the conventional spokes; and even the numbering system was new. The firebox was of all welded construction and the valve gear housed between the frames was enclosed in an enormous oil bath. These were but a few of the innovations which were part of the Southern Railway's first mainline Pacific tender engines. Some of the ideas proved to be sound but others made the engines prone to failure. The entire class of 30 engines were rebuilt to more orthodox principles by British Railways and they then became thoroughly reliable and speedy machines.

**87.** The Peppercorn Pacifics of the Eastern Region of British Railways were the final development of the Gresley 4–6–2s. The first of the class emerged from Doncaster Works in the final month before the railways were nationalised, the remaining additions being built under B.R. auspices. Regretably, none of these A1 Class engines survived for preservation although 50 were built. They were only 15 years old when condemned. This picture shows 60144 *King's Courier*.

**88.** British Railways undertook extensive trials of the various locomotives from the "Big Four" and from the results standard classes of engines were built using the best ideas from each. Thus was born the Britannia Class Pacifics which were introduced in 1951. The decision was taken in 1958 to supersede steam with electric and diesel traction, and by 1968 all the Britannia Class Pacifics had gone. This illustration shows No. 70023 *Venus*.

# 0–8–0

A natural development of the 0–6–0. The type first appeared on the Barry Railway in the late 1880's, but the L.N.W.R. put 0–8–0's into mass production from 1892 with F.W. Webb's 2-cylinder compounds. 0–8–0's were first and foremost mineral traffic locomotives capable of hauling heavy trains at moderate speeds.

**89.** L.N.W.R. 0–8–0 Class G2 locomotive No. 9419 was built at Crewe in 1921. These engines were the last of a series of 0–8–0's constructed at Crewe begun by F. W. Webb and ending with the design of Bowen-Cooke in 1912. They were robust machines and many lasted well into the British Railways era and the demise of steam in 1968. They were known as Super D's or Duck Eights to loco-spotters (duck = 0). They had a most distinctive exhaust beat and could pull enormous trains but could never be hurried.

**90.** Class 7F No. 9500, was the first of a series of 175 engines with which the L.M.S. hoped to replace the Super D's. Building commenced in 1929 and the design was based on the Standard Midland 0–6–0, but they inherited the inadequate axle problems of their smaller counterparts and failed to come up to expectations. All of the Austin Sevens, as they were known, had gone for scrap long before the Duck Eights.

**91.** Maunsell's Class Z 0–8–0T for the Southern Railway, was built in 1929 and No. 955 was one of the class of eight. They saw service in the marshalling yards as heavy shunting engines, and also as banking engines assisting trains up the severe incline which separates Exeter St. David's and Central Stations.

# 2–8–0

They were known generally as Consolidations and were an extension of the 0–8–0's having an additional axle (pony truck) at the leading end. This provided a better lead into curved track and also permitted the use of longer frames to support extended boilers.

**92.** J. G. Robinson's Class 8K for the Great Central Railway was first built at Gorton in 1911, but the design was so successful that it was adopted by the R.O.D. for mass production during the First World War. At the cessation of hostilities in 1918 a large number of these robust machines were made available for purchase or for hire to British railways. In 1919 the asking price for an engine and tender was £10,000, with stocks still in hand in 1928 the price had fallen to £340! They could therefore be seen almost anywhere in Great Britain, some went overseas to China and Australia.

**93.** Some were purchased by the Great Western Railway in 1919, they were fitted with G.W. boiler mountings and details and generally ''Swindonised''.

**94.** In 1935 William Stanier's 2–8–0 emerged from Crewe Works, history repeating itself shortly after as with the Robinson 8K's in 1914. Stanier's 8F's became the War Office Locomotive in 1939 and saw them being constructed at Brighton, Doncaster and Darlington Locomotive Works. At the end of the war some went to L.N.E.R. stock and became Class 06. The L.M.S. had a total of 663 of these very useful engines.

**95.** The 1939-45 War also saw the introduction of an Austerity Locomotive designed by Mr. R. A. Riddles, Deputy Director-General of Royal Engineer Equipment. They were based on the Stanier 8F's but had parallel boilers in place of the taper boilers of their Crewe counterparts. 733 of these WD's became British Railway property in 1948. No. 90425 was built by Vulcan Foundry in September 1943.

**96.** No. 2832 is an example of G. J. Churchward's 28XX Class 2–8–0 freight engine for the G.W.R., the first of which was built in 1903.

**97.** Also from Swindon in 1910, a series of 2–8–0T's were built for the heavy coal traffic in and around South Wales. No. 4227 is a 42XX Class locomotive.

**98.** The only examples of the 2–8–0 type to be built by the Midland Railway at Derby were the special freight engines employed on the difficult route of the Somerset and Dorset Railway. No. 53805 was one of a batch of eleven which first appeared in 1914. They were extremely capable machines and, in the final years of the S & D., were often utilised on express passenger trains between Bath and Bournemouth on busy Saturdays in summer.

# 0–10–0

**99.** Trains travelling on the Midland Railway route between Bristol and Birmingham were confronted with the formidable 2 mile long 1 in 38 Lickey Incline at Bromsgrove. Trains were given rear end assistance over this obstacle and the mammoth 0–10–0 was designed and built at Derby for this purpose. Known always as Big Bertha, it was capable of doing the work of two engines in one sustained effort. Weighing in at 73 tons 13 cwt with 4 cylinders it was the largest engine to be built by the Midland Railway. Originally numbered 2290, it became 58100 on British Railways.

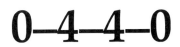

0–4–4–0

**100.** The Fairlie Patent double engine of the Ffestiniog Railway, one of the narrow gauge Welsh railways. Robert Fairlie in effect put two engines back to back with a common firebox, the ingenious invention originating in 1869. The first engine was named *Little Wonder* and was used to convey the slate trains between Blaenau Ffestiniog and Portmadog. Engines of the type are working the same line today, but as a major tourist attraction hauling passenger trains between the sea and the mountains of Snowdonia.